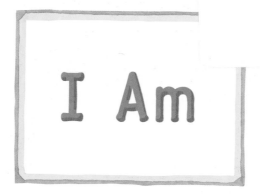

I Am

by Lisa Kindrey   illustrated by Stephanie Peterson

Orlando   Boston   Dallas   Chicago   San Diego

Visit *The Learning Site!*

www.harcourtschool.com

Printed in China

ISBN 0-15-325409-2

10 121 10 09 08 07 06 05

Ordering Options
ISBN 0-15-323766-X (Collection)
ISBN 0-15-329525-2 (package of 5)

I am blue.

I am red.

I am green.

I am yellow.

I am purple.

I am orange.